Jeanne Wakatsuki Houston's

Farewell to Manzanar

BookCaps Study Guide

Table of Contents

Historical Context

Jeanne Wakatsuki was born in 1934 and raised in California. She graduated from San Jose State University in 1956 with a degree in Journalism, and only one year later she married John Houston who was also a writer. John joined the Air Force and his duties took he and Jeanne to England and then France where she was able to study French civilization.

Wakatsuki has been praised for her many political and historical writings, but "Farewell to Manzanar" is her most well-known. It documents her experiences with her family during the three years that they spent held captive in a desert in Southeast California at the Manzanar Relocation Center.

The novel explains what happened after the Japanese attacked Pearl Harbor during World War II in 1942. People of Japanese descent who were living in the United States were treated as enemies and held as prisoners in relocation camps, the Wakatsuki family included.

The Japanese and other Asians had been distrusted and unwelcome by Americans since the first Chinese immigrated into the country in the mid-nineteenth century, but the prejudice had died down some until the Pearl Harbor attack. Many Asians gave birth to children while in America, which made their children official United States citizens, though that did not stop them from being thrown into the relocation camps.

The Manzanar camps housed over 11,000 people within eight buildings while they existed. In 1944, the camps were ordered by the government to be shut down because they housed Nisei, Asians who were born in the United States and thus citizens, but it took an entire year for the camps to completely disappear.

Those who survived living in the camps demanded compensation from the government for unlawful imprisonment, and finally, in 1988, each survivor was awarded $20,000. President George Bush issued a public apology to the survivors in 1990, and, in 1992, he declared that Manzanar be deemed a National Historical Site.

Plot

"Farewell to Manzanar" recounts author Jeanne Wakatsuki Houston's life as a young Japanese-American girl in the wake of the Pearl Harbor attacks. Jeanne's father was a sardine fisherman and his boat had just gone out to sea when word came that the Japanese had struck Pearl Harbor. Immediately, Jeanne's father rushes home to burn his Japanese flag, and identification papers, but it is no use as he is caught by the FBI.

Jeanne's Mama tries to run with the children but soon President Roosevelt gives the word to relocate all potential threats to national security and the Japanese are moved into relocation camps, including the Wakatsuki family.

The conditions at Manzanar Relocation Camp are poor, and people fall ill, and are emotionally weakened. The family begins to fall apart, Jeanne becomes religious, and Papa is arrested. When he returns he is a changed man and resorts to drinking and violence, almost striking Mama at one point. Those who help the government are referred to as "inu" or traitors and are looked down upon by the other members of the camp.

One search for an inu results in what is referred to as the December Riot and leads to the US government asking the Japanese camp members to take an oath that will swear their loyalty to the United States. Many men refuse, but Papa agrees to it, and soon the family is moved to a much nicer barracks, and camp begins to resemble a real town, with schools and activities.

In December of 1944 President Roosevelt orders that the camps be shut down and soon Papa and the rest of the family head to Long Beach in a blue sedan. The family, especially Jeanne, experience silent prejudice in Long Beach and Jeanne nearly drops out of school. When the family finally moves to San Jose Jeanne fits in more with the other students and begins to discover who she is. In 1972 Jeanne visits Manzanar with her husband and two children, afraid that if she does not see the place with her own eyes then she will start to believe it never existed.

Characters

Jeanne Wakatsuki

Jeanne is the narrator and author of "Farewell to Manzanar" and was just seven years old at the start of the story. She is the youngest of ten children and is her father's obvious favorite. Jeanne is greatly influenced by Papa, despite the fact that she grows to despise him for his traditionalism, and she becomes a rebel just like him. She keeps herself busy at camp by trying new things and has a hard time fitting in and being accepted after camp life is over and she begins to attend a regular high school. Jeanne struggles to find herself through her adolescence and decide who she truly is without conforming to anyone's opinions of who she should be other than her own.

Papa (George Ko Wakatsuki)

Papa is Jeanne's father and is married to Mama. When he was just a young man Papa abandoned his family's idea that he should enter the military and become a warrior and instead fled to the US. He planned to become a lawyer but ended up making his life farming and fishing. He eloped with Mama, and they traveled all over the country together, having ten children along the way. Papa struggles with embracing his Japanese heritage and having pride in it, when he knows that Japan will lose the war and he abandoned the country so long ago. Papa becomes an abusive alcoholic after he is imprisoned and accused of being a spy for the Japanese.

Mama (Rigu Sukai Wakatsuki)

Mama is Jeanne's mother and is married to Papa. As a girl growing up in Washington, she was promised in marriage to a farmer when she met Papa, and the two eloped. After Papa is imprisoned Mama takes over the role as head of the family and does her best to keep them together. Despite her discomfort in the living situation at camp, she retains her dignity and remains patient and collected because those are qualities she holds in high regard. Mama never gives up on Papa through his alcoholism and manages to support the family after camp shuts down until Papa pulls himself together and gets a job.

Woody (Woodrow Wakatsuki)

Woody is twenty-four years of age and one of the oldest children in the family and he takes on a leadership role while Papa is gone. Woody is level-headed and reasonable and acts as a fatherly figure toward Jeanne and the other siblings in Papa's absence. Despite Papa's protests against it, Woody joins the US military believing that the more people who join, the faster the war will come to an end. Papa convinces Woody to wait to be drafted, rather than volunteering but still Woody's participation solidifies his support of the United States. Woody visits Papa's family in Hiroshima as a part of the US military so he can try to understand Papa better.

Kiyo Wakatsuki

Kiyo is the second youngest child in the family, next to Jeanne. Kiyo and Jeanne are very close and spend much of their time together. Kiyo and Jeanne go through a few tough experiences together, such as the time they are spat on and called "dirty japs" and the time they are nearly attacked in the ghetto on Terminal Island by a group of children. Kiyo saves Mama from being hit by Papa in one of his drunken rages by coming out from where he was hiding and punching Papa in the face. Kiyo hides from Papa for two weeks after the incident though Papa forgives him right away.

Eleanor Wakatsuki

Eleanor is one of the older children in the family. Eleanor and her husband move away from camp when given the option, relocating to Reno, Nevada. Eleanor's husband, Shig, is drafted into the US military while Eleanor is pregnant. She returns to camp to live with the rest of the family as she cannot stay in Reno alone while he is gone. Soon after returning to camp Eleanor goes into labor, which worries Mama and Papa as two of their other children have hemorrhaged during labor, and one of them died. Eleanor is fine and gives birth to a baby boy. The birth is such a happy occasion that it brings Mama and Papa back together and ends their fighting.

Radine

Radine is a blond-haired white girl whose family is from Texas. Jeanne meets Radine when she enrolls in school, in Long Beach, after being released from Manzanar. Radine is shocked when she finds out that Jeanne can speak English, and despite her initial prejudice, she and Jeanne become great friends. Radine and Jeanne are a lot alike and even have the same taste in boys, though friction occurs between the girls when the boys Jeanne likes go for Radine because Jeanne is Japanese. Radine also gets preferential treatment in the band because she is white and Jeanne almost is not even allowed in.

Bill Wakatsuki

Bill is the oldest child of the Wakatsuki family. He and Woody are the two sons who work on Papa's fishing boat with him at the start of the story. Bill remains in camp with the family though he distances himself from them. He makes friends with other men his age and begins to go off and eat meals with them, realizing that the food in other mess halls is better than it is in the one closest to the Wakatsuki barracks. Bill joins and becomes the leader of a dance group called "The Jive Bombers".

Aunt Toyo

Aunt Toyo is Papa's aunt who lives in Hiroshima. After the war ends, Woody goes to Hiroshima on a peace mission for the US military, and while there he visits Aunt Toyo and the rest of Papa's family. Aunt Toyo welcomes Woody graciously to her home, and, despite the fact that her family is very poor, she prepares a grand meal for Woody on her finest china and puts him to sleep on her finest linens. Woody thinks that Papa would be proud of the way Aunt Toyo treated him, and he understands where Papa gets his pride from. Aunt Toyo cries next to Woody's bed when she realizes how much he resembles Ko.

Granny

Granny is the aging mother of Mama. She is sixty-five years old and was born in Japan. Granny is very nearly blind and is becoming quite frail, to the point where Mama has to deliver Granny's meals for her as she cannot leave the barracks. There is often a scuffle to get food in the mess hall and Granny cannot handle the commotion. Granny does not speak English as she has refused to learn the language. She has much pride in Japan and prizes the few belongings she still has that have come from her native country.

Chizu

Chizu is Woody's wife. She is one of the people at the start of the story who is standing on the pier with Jeanne, waving to Papa, Woody, and Bill as they set out on their fishing excursion the day Pearl Harbor is attacked. Chizu is the mother of a daughter as well as a son who was born at Manzanar. Chizu helps Mama in caring for the younger children and takes on a motherly role in their lives. She is often the person to make peace when there is fighting and to distract the children from Papa's drunken rages.

Kaz

Kaz is married to Jeanne's sister, Martha. Kaz is a part of a team that checks the reservoirs in the area. On the night of the December, Riot Kaz and his crew are checking a reservoir and camping for the night when they are bombarded by military police who suspect they are on the run, especially when they see the men are armed with ax handles. Kaz explains that they are not on the run but are part of a reservoir crew from Manzanar and the ax handles are for protection against the rioters. The general goes to Manzanar to check out Kaz's story and finds that he is telling the truth and Kaz, and his men are set free.

Leonard Rodriguez

Leonard is a boy that Jeanne attends school with when her family moves to San Jose. When Jeanne is nominated to be carnival queen and shows up wearing a sarong the applause makes it obvious that she will win the election. Leonard overhears a teachers' plan to stuff the ballot box so another girl, who is white, will win over Jeanne. Leonard accuses the teachers of prejudice because Jeanne is Japanese American and tells them that he will expose their plan if they go through with it. Because of Leonard's foiling of the plan, Jeanne is crowned carnival queen.

Fred Tayama

Fred is the leader of the Japanese American Citizens League at Manzanar. It is suspected that Fred is in league with the US government and is feeding them information and going against his own people. Because of Fred's suspected involvement with the Americans he is severely beaten and his attackers are arrested. The campers at Manzanar, in protest of the arrests, start a riot which becomes known as the December Riot. Sometime during the night when the riot is taking place, a group of men decide to go to the hospital and finish off Fred Tayama.

Sister Bernadette

Sister Bernadette is a Canadian-Japanese nun who Jeanne speaks to about religion. Jeanne is very interested in the idea of religion, martyrs, and suffering and wants to learn more and to participate though Papa will not allow her. Sister Bernadette comes to the Wakatsuki barracks to speak with Papa about Jeanne being baptized, as it is what Jeanne wishes, but Papa explains that Jeanne is not old enough to understand what baptism means and also if she is baptized she will no longer be able to marry a Japanese man.

Themes

Injustice

In the wake of the Pearl Harbor attack, the US became anti-Japanese, scared that anyone Japanese could be working with the enemy and so all Japanese living in America were sent to relocation camps. In the relocation camps, they were forced to live in extremely poor conditions, especially at first, and were treated as though they were animals. Some of the Japanese living in the camps were actually Nisei, meaning they were Japanese who were born in America and, therefore, American citizens, meaning that the US were imprisoning their own citizens in the camps. It took three Supreme Court cases to rule the camps as illegal, and shut them down, but much injustice was carried out in the three years they were open.

Prejudice

After the Pearl Harbor attacks, the Japanese Americans were seen as dangerous to the general public which is why they were put into camps. Once the camps shut down, and the Japanese were allowed to return to society they had to deal with prejudice from the outside world. While people did not outwardly discriminate, or find the Japanese as threats any longer they did make assumptions and form stereotypes about them; one example of this is when Jeanne was asked to read aloud in school, and the other students were shocked that she spoke English, obviously not realizing that she was a US citizen.

Disintegration of Family

While in the Manzanar camp the Wakatsuki family slowly began to fall apart, which weighed most heavily on Jeanne as she was so young and unable to run away as her other siblings could. The family slowly started eating in separate places, something they had never done before they were sent to the camp, and then began participating in different activities, some joined the military, and some just moved away. By the end of camp, Jeanne completely resents Papa for not allowing her to do what she wants and when they get home he will not allow to her to fit in with everyone else, feeling she should be "more Japanese". Jeanne blames Papa for the disintegration of her family.

Identity

It is Jeanne and Papa who have the most difficult time with identity, despite the fact that Papa seems to know exactly who he is. Papa knows he is Japanese and should respect his ancestry by holding on to his heritage, but he becomes an abusive alcoholic who cannot hold down a job due to his pride, alluding to his confusion with his place in life, and finding somewhere he belongs after camp. Jeanne is in her teen years and tries out everything new she can find: baton twirling, religion, glee club, and dance to name a few. Papa insists that Jeanne stay true to her heritage, but Jeanne wants nothing more than to be accepted. In high school, outside of Manzanar, Jeanne has a hard time knowing who she is and how she should present herself.

Loyalty

Loyalty is something that the relocated Japanese having a problem dealing with because they feel as though they should remain loyal to their own heritage yet the US are pressuring them to admit their loyalty to America during the war. When asked to take an oath pledging their loyalty and their willingness to serve in the war many of the Japanese do not know what to do, though the majority wishes to remain loyal to their Japanese roots. Papa is ostracized for his desire to pledge his loyalty to the US but only because he think it will make life easier for his family, and it does. It is obvious throughout the novel that while Papa ran from Japan as a young man he still has much respect for the culture and his family in Hiroshima.

Freedom

Freedom is a difficult concept for some to grasp when the relocation camps are closed down, especially Papa. Many of the Japanese have nowhere to go when the camps close and are worried they will not be able to find a home. Papa wishes to allow the government to decide where his family will go, as he is having a hard time dealing with freedom. Jeanne likens her father's attitude to that of a slave who has just been given freedom; they have been slaves for so long they do not know what to do with freedom once they have it.

Survival

The Japanese Americans go from a state of living comfortable lives to having everything ripped out from under them and being forced to make do with what they can find or are given. Many families are forced to move several times before they are finally put into relocation camps like Manzanar, and once they arrive in the camps they are presented with living conditions that are barely fit for animals. They are forced to live in cramped quarters that are dirty, and cold and the toilets have no privacy. Rather than keep families together the camps pull them apart because survival becomes "every man for himself".

Resilience

Jeanne is the character that has the most resilience, or even bothers to bounce back. After being released from camp Mama does what she needs to do to protect the family and Papa mopes for a little while before deciding he wants to be a farmer again, but Jeanne struggles to find herself. In high school Jeanne is discriminated against by teachers and students alike to the point where she almost drops out though she decides to keep pushing forward in a new school. In her new school, she is torn between what her father wants her to be, what will get her accepted by the other students, and who she truly is. Jeanne does not want to be someone else, and she does not want to change the fact that her face is Japanese, she simply wants to be accepted the way she is. She realizes that because of her Japanese face the white girls will never be her friends no matter what she does. Jeanne always bounces back and keeps moving forward despite her obstacles.

Rebellion

Jeanne rebels mostly against Papa because he is the one who is trying to force her to be a certain person rather than allowing her to explore the possibilities of life. Jeanne rebels against Papa by taking baton lessons, practicing religion and nearly getting baptized, joining glee club, making friends with the other minorities in her neighborhood after leaving camp, using her sexuality to attract the attention of white boys, and becomes best friends with a white girl. Even into adulthood Jeanne challenges Papa's values as she marries a man who is not Japanese. Jeanne did not use rebellion as a means for attention so much as a way to discover who she is and to feel as though she is accepted for the first time in her life.

Reasoning

The Wakatsuki men do nothing on a whim but reason through their decisions before making them. Papa decides to answer "yes" to the oath despite the fact that the other camp members call him "inu" for it and think he is working with the US government. He realizes that Japan will lose the war and whether he is truly loyal to the US or not it is smart for him to make them believe he is. Woody awaits the draft, despite the fact that Papa does not want him to serve in the military. Woody reasons with Papa that though he respects his Japanese ancestry they are going to lose the war and every person who joins the fight brings it closer to ending and thus closer to the camps being shut down.

Chapter Summaries

Chapter One

It is Sunday December 7, 1941, and Jeanne Wakatsuki is seven years old. She, her mother (Mama), and her sister-in-law Chizu watch from the docks as Jeanne's father, Papa, and two brothers, Bill and Woody prepare their sardine boat for a fishing trip. Papa has two boats, which he pays for by sharing some of the fish, he catches with the local canneries on Terminal Island near Long Beach. Jeanne, Mama, and Chizu watch from the dock as the boats take off, waving until they can hardly see them anymore. Suddenly the boats stop in the water and turn around; Mama is worried that something has happened. A man from the cannery comes out to tell the ladies that the Japanese have bombed Pearl Harbor but Jeanne and Mama are confused as neither knows what Pearl Harbor is. When Papa returns he immediately burns his Japanese flag and destroys his identification, both of which tie him to Japan. As Papa is not a US citizen, and he has a fishing license he is seen as a potential spy and those are the type of people the FBI are looking for. Two weeks later, while the family is staying with Woody on Terminal Island, Papa is arrested by the FBI who are questioning many Japanese people and searching homes for any items that could be used for spying. The family does not know where Papa is taken, but the newspaper the next day says that Papa has been arrested for supplying oil to Japanese submarines. Mama is distraught and depressed, but Jeanne does not understand why until one year later when she finally sees Papa again.

Chapter Two

After Papa is arrested the family moves to the Japanese projects at Terminal Island. Jeanne feels uncomfortable in her new surroundings because she has never been around so many other Japanese people before and she remembers a time when Papa used to tell her he would "sell her to the Chinamen" if she misbehaved. The other young people often caused problems and bully Jeanne and her brother, Kiyo, because they do not speak Japanese. Jeanne and her family stay there for two months until the government decides that the Japanese need to be moved further from Long Beach. Mama moves the family, including sixty-five year old Granny, to the Boyle Heights ghetto in Los Angeles. Soon after settling in the Japanese population began to hear rumors that President Roosevelt was going to order that the Japanese be relocated as they are threats to national security. Mama receives a letter from Papa, and the kids enroll in school. Jeanne does not like school because her teacher is the first Caucasian she has encountered who has acted hostile toward the Japanese. As the feeling toward the Japanese throughout the country turns fearful, the government orders that the Wakatsuki family be sent to a relocation camp at Manzanar, along with many other Japanese. They are picked up by buses and given tags to pin to their collars along with identification numbers. Once they arrive at the camp they are horrified at the food they are given and their living conditions. They are served rice with canned apricots over it, though the Japanese never mix anything sweet with their rice. All twelve family members are given only two rooms to share and must make mattresses out of straw and try to divide their space with blankets. Some of the couples have a difficult time being in such close quarters to the others, though Jeanne does not mind it. Jeanne's sister and her husband soon leave for Idaho.

Chapter Three

After the first night spent in Manzanar, the Wakatsuki
family wakes up covered in grey dust that has blown
through the cracks in the walls. In order to stay warm,
they had all covered up with whatever extra clothing
they had with them, and because of the dust it is all
filthy. Jeanne and Kiyo think that it is funny that they
are all covered in dust, but Mama is frustrated.
Woody asks from the next room whether they all fell
into the flour barrel as he did. The family soon gets to
cleaning up; Ray and Kiyo cover the knotholes while
Jeanne and May sweep and fold the clothes. Woody
tells the boys that if any sand makes it through the
knotholes he will make them eat it. Kiyo asks about
the sand and Woody jokingly says that it is a different
type of sand. Despite the knotholes being covered the
sand still comes through the cracks in the floor and
walls when the wind blows so Mama asks Woody to
patch the cracks. Mama is very displeased with the
living conditions, as it is something she is not used to
and feels they do not deserve. As the family heads out
for breakfast, the boys joke about what they may be
eating; perhaps rice covered in maple syrup or
pancakes with soy sauce.

Chapter Four

The family is forced to wait outside in the cold for breakfast, for an hour and a half. When they finally do get to eat they do so huddled around an oil heater for warmth. Woody fixes things he finds around camp to make the family's life easier but they do not feel comfortable in their new home for months. Jeanne states that while they were not ready for the camps she does not think that the camps were ready for the Japanese either. The family did not bring warm enough clothing, as they underestimated the weather conditions they would encounter being in a higher altitude. Surplus is sent in by the War Department thought it is much too large for the Japanese people, so they set up their own clothing company and modify the surplus to be suitable for them. The camps are broken down, and the conditions are horrendous. Everyone falls ill from time to time from immunizations and spoiled food, causing the "Manzanar runs". The latrine nearest the Wakatsuki's is overflowing so they are forced to visit another latrine. The toilets are back to back with no partitions, which is upsetting to everyone, especially Mama. An older lady uses a cardboard box to serve as a partition and is kind enough to share it with Mama. The cardboard makeshift partitions are used by many people until read partitions arrive, but even with the partitions many people never get used to the lack of privacy that the latrines bring, Mama being one of them.

Chapter Five

After a few weeks at Manzanar, Jeanne notices that her family has stopped eating together in the mess halls. Granny has gotten too old to travel to the mess hall, the older boys eat with their friends in other mess halls that have better food, the younger boys try to eat in as many mess halls as they can within each meal period, and Jeanne and Kiyo usually eat away from the adults. Camp life disintegrated family closeness, despite the efforts to keep the families together. Jeanne notes that after the camps closed the disintegration only got worse because the older children moved out of the home and the rest of the family members were crammed into tiny apartments that made them miserable. At the camp, the men begin to volunteer for any jobs they hear of doing manual labor and Mama becomes a dietician for the hospital where she makes only nineteen dollars per month that she sends to Los Angeles to pay for the warehouse where the family's furniture is stored. Mama becomes preoccupied with worrying about Papa and begins to ignore Jeanne. Jeanne becomes a people-watcher and is interested in the different types of people she sees wandering around camp, especially the nuns and priest who try to convert her to Catholicism. She walks around in the sun, and pretends she is a martyr, but Papa makes her stop one day when her walks in the sun give her sunstroke. Papa has just returned from being imprisoned, and, on the day he arrived, everyone met him at the station. When he gets off the bus they notice that he is very frail and has a bad leg, which causes him to use the aid of a cane when he walks. Everyone is scared to approach him except for Jeanne who runs to him and hugs him tearfully.

Chapter Six

As Papa recovers he still uses his cane, only instead of using it to help him walk he swats family members with it. This makes Jeanne think of the ancient samurai swords that Papa's warrior ancestors used. Papa's family were samurai who had their status as warriors taken away from them by Commodore Matthew Perry. Papa entered military school at the urging of his uncle, but when he was seventeen he dropped out and fled to Hawaii. He heard about a job there, spent what little money he had on a suit, and went to interview only to find out that it was on a cane field, something he was not interesting in. Papa went to Idaho to be a houseboy for a lawyer and after five years enrolled in law school at the University of Idaho. When he met Mama he changed his plans. Mama was born to a cane worker in Hawaii but grew up in Washington. She had already been promised to someone else for marriage, but when she met Papa they ran away together and got married in Oregon. Over the next eighteen years, the family moved around while Papa took on odd jobs, and they had ten children. After the Great Depression, the family moved to Santa Monica where Papa acquired his two boats and began fishing for a living. Jeanne remembers her parents being at their happiest at their golden wedding anniversary. She says that her father was not what one would consider "great" but he was a passionate dreamer and did everything with vigor. The other men who were held with Papa at the detention camp in Fort Lincoln remember him because he was always helpful and taught the other men English.

Chapter Seven

When Papa is at Fort Lincoln he is interrogated by a man who wants to know if Papa has had any contact with his uncle in Japan and also the names of all Papa's children. Papa tells the man that he cannot return to Japan because he is the outcast of his family and he names all of his children except Jeanne, explaining that he has too many children to remember them all. The interrogator explains to Papa that he was taken in for supplying oil to the Japanese submarines, though Papa denies these claims. The interrogator asks what is in the drums on Papa's boat if it is not oil, and he explains that it is fish guts, which he uses to attract his catch. When asked how he feels about what happened in Pearl Harbor Papa says he is sad for both countries, but the Americans will likely win because they are bigger and stronger and the leaders of Japan are not very smart. The interrogator asks Papa if he is still loyal to Japan, and Papa explains to the man that he has been in American for nine years longer than the interrogator has been alive, and he is still not allowed citizenship. He does not answer the question, but he asks the interrogator what he would want if his own parents were involved; would he want them to fight to the death or to just give up?

Chapter Eight

Papa moves in with the rest of the family in their crowded barracks and does not venture back outside for a very long time. Mama delivers Papa's meals to him from the mess hall and even uses the extra rice and fruit to make her own brandy and wine. Papa spends all of his time drinking, vomiting, and lashing out at his family members. The reason Papa never leaves is because he feels as though he is better than everyone else, but Mama finds out that others do not see him that one but see him as a traitor; she overhears some women talking who refer to Papa as "inu" which means "dog" or "informant" in Japanese. They believe he is inu because he left Fort Lincoln earlier than the other men and they assume he managed the early release by becoming an informant for the Americans. Mama tells Papa of the allegations and he flies into a drunken rage. He yells at her for not bringing him any food and for participating in the gossip that is going around camp about him which he says is the reason he stays inside all day. Papa tells Mama he is going to kill her and raises his cane, to which she encourages him to hit her, but before he can Kiyo pops out from where he is hiding and punches Papa in the face. Jeanne feels proud of Kiyo for standing up for Mama but still feels as though her entire world is crumbling. Kiyo hides for a couple weeks before he asks for Papa's forgiveness, which he is given. Papa does not change, however, and still spends his days getting drunk and acting abusive toward Mama.

Chapter Nine

Papa is humiliated by the rumors being spread about him and deals with his humiliation by lashing out against those around him. The other men are frustrated as well, but their frustration does not come out until the December Riot. In the months that lead up to the Riot, the people who live at Manzanar becomes increasingly vocal about the poor living conditions and the quality of food they are served. There are meetings in the mess hall where the residents discuss these issues, along with their desire for better wages. There is much violence in the wake of these discussions which culminate in an attack on Fred Tayama, head of the Japanese American Citizens League on December 5, 1942. Three men are arrested in conjunction with this attack, one of them a kitchen worker who has been trying to arrange a union and has been known to throw out accusations of the chief steward selling food on the black market. When he is arrested the Riot begins, and Papa does not participate, instead keeping all of the family inside the barracks. He says that the rioters are idiots, but Mama understands them, telling Papa they are treated like animals and are sick of it. To end the riot the authorities say they will bring the cook back to camp, but there are already 2,000 people rioting and the security workers are nowhere to be found. One of the rioters leaves to release the cook from jail and some others head to the hospital to finish what they started with Frank Tayama. A group of rioters throws rocks at the military police, and the police respond with tear gas, and even open fire with machine guns, killing two of the Japanese and injuring others. The bells from the mess hall begin to ring that night and do not stop until the next day.

Chapter Ten

Kaz, Jeanne's brother-in-law, heads a reservoir maintenance team at Manzanar. On the night of the riots, they are sent out if camp and given ax handles for protection in case someone discovers that they are working with the administration. Kaz's crew checks the reservoir and sets up camp for their twenty-four hour shift. While Kaz is lying in bed, he sees a shadow pass by the window, and immediately after the camp is stormed by military police who think that they have discovered some rogue Japanese and hold them up with guns. The sergeant asks Kaz and the others what they are doing, still suspicious after Kaz explains to them that they are from Manzanar and are working on the reservoirs. The sergeant wonders why they are armed with ax handles and Kaz explains to him that they were given the handles for protection and perhaps the sergeant should go to Manzanar where someone can corroborate the story. While the sergeant is gone Kaz and his crew stare at the military police, both groups wary of one another. When the sergeant returns he confirms Kaz's story and tells the police they can be on their way.

Chapter Eleven

The camp director tries to keep everyone's spirits up during the holidays by giving everyone a Christmas tree, but Jeanne ends up disappointed anyway because there are no good presents, and Papa is always drunk. By February, there is a lot of tension around camp because the government makes everyone who is over seventeen take an oath of loyalty. There are two questions everyone is expected to answer "yes" to, regarding whether they would serve in the US military and whether they would pledge their allegiance to the US over Japan. There is a lot of debate and friction amongst the people living in camp over whether to take the oath. Woody says he would be willing to fight, but Papa tells him that a man must agree with what he is fighting for. No one knows what to do because if they answer "yes" to the questions they will be put into the US military but if they answer "no" then they will be sent back to Japan, so they cannot win either way. They have a third option to relocate their family away from the west coast if they have a sponsor somewhere else. Papa decides that he must answer "yes" because he is sure that America will win the war and he has no intention of being sent back to Japan. Nearly everyone in camp wants to say "no" and when a meeting is held to discuss everyone answering "no" collectively Papa strikes up some controversy by telling them he plans to answer "yes", which leads to the talk of him being an inu again. A scuffle arises, and Jeanne sees Papa attack another man. Back at the barracks Papa is silent until one of Chizu's friends arrives and sings the national anthem of Japan with him, which makes him cry.

Chapter Twelve

In the springtime of 1943, the family is moved to a nicer barracks near an old pear orchard. The name "manzanar" actually means "apple orchard" and Jeanne explains that the area surrounding the camp used to be full of orchards. Papa is given a job where he tends to the fruit trees, and Mama is much closer to her job at the hospital. The living conditions are much nicer and larger in the new barracks as there are ceilings, and linoleum flooring so the dust does not come in the way it did in the old barracks. Papa begins to drink less because he spends a lot of time outdoors, though he does still drink some. The Japanese are allowed more freedom after their first year in the camp, and this leads Papa to spend time hiking and exploring his creative side by building furniture and painting. Those who live in the barracks take on an attitude of "shikata ga nai" which means "it cannot be helped" and thus the mood in camp is calm and subdued. People begin to plant gardens and even create a farm. There are churches, movie theaters, schools, and stores built and life becomes normal with the camp operating as its own town. Woody considers volunteering for the military, but Papa convinces him not to and so Woody waits to be drafted and works at the general store in the meantime. Kiyo spends his time looking for arrowheads that he sells to old men and Ray joins a football team that has been started. Jillian and Bill, Jeanne's older brother and sister, join a hillbilly band and a dancing band that entertain the people in the camp and are featured in the Manzanar high school yearbook for 1943-1944.

Chapter Thirteen

The authorities in camp build schools for all ages and Jeanne is enrolled in the fourth grade. Jeanne really likes her teacher who is a single woman from Kentucky and she also becomes a member of the glee club which performs all over camp. The relocation department starts a recreation program and brings in some Quakers to run it. The recreation department plans hiking trips to camp sites, and one of the Quaker girls has a crush on a Japanese boy she plans an overnight camping trip, so they can spend time together. Jeanne likes going on the hikes but gets nervous when she spends too much time away from camp. She decides she wants to join the baton club at school, so she takes baton-twirling lessons, and practices for months. Jeanne is more interested in the American activity of baton-twirling than she was in the dance lessons she took with a Geisha because she did not understand the Japanese traditions and dialect. She also tried to take ballet lessons but did not like her teacher, whom she describes as out of shape. Jeanne becomes interested in religion again and expresses a desire to be baptized, an idea which Papa vehemently refuses because he says Jeanne will no longer be able to marry a Japanese man if she goes through with it. One of the nuns tries to talk to Papa about the baptism, but he still refuses, maintaining that Jeanne is too young to understand it. Jeanne gets mad at Papa for his refusal and goes back to her baton-twirling hobby.

Chapter Fourteen

In retrospect Jeanne agrees with her father's decision to not allow her to be baptized, though at the time she grew further away from him because of it as she did not think he understood her or wanted her to be happy. Eleanor, who had moved away from camp with her husband, ends up moving back because she is about to have their baby and he has been drafted into the war. While Eleanor is in labor the family worries about her because Jeanne's other two older sisters hemorrhaged badly when they were giving birth, and there is not much blood around camp for a transfusion. One of the sisters was able to take a transfusion from Woody, but the other one did not survive. Into Eleanor's second day in labor, either Mama or Papa sits with her every minute of the day. During the afternoon, of Eleanor's second day in labor Mama runs through the firebreak toward Papa which worries him because she had been sitting with Eleanor. Mama, however, is delivering the happy news that Eleanor has just given birth to a healthy baby boy. Mama and Papa both cry with happiness, but Jeanne does not feel anything about the birth of her nephew. She feels very out standing on the outside while her parents share such a tender and emotional moment.

Chapter Fifteen

After the birth of Eleanor's son, Mama and Papa become increasingly closer than they had been in previous months. Despite Mama and Papa reconciling the family does not grow closer together as the older children in the family all choose to join the military or relocate, pulling the family further apart. By the time 1944 comes around, there are only 6,000 people left in the camp, and those people are mostly elderly or children. Eleanor leaves camp to go back to Reno and stay with friends until her husband gets out of the military. That year Woody is finally drafted and despite the fact that Papa urges him to refuse service he reports to duty in November when he is called in. The family sees Woody off when he leaves, but Jeanne does not comprehend where he is going, just as she did not understand where Papa was going when he was arrested. Jeanne is reminded of the day she, Mama, and Chizu waved goodbye to Papa's fleet the day the war began only now there are many more people waving goodbye. Woody is a part of the 442nd combat regiment which is all-Nisei, which means it is comprised of all Japanese who were born in America. The regiment is very famous and Jeanne states that one of the women in camp had just received a Medal of Honor for her son who was killed while serving in Italy. As more people begin to join the military, families are split up, which worries everyone because they wonder what state their families will be in after the war is over.

Chapter Sixteen

In December 1944 the Supreme Court finally rules that the Japanese relocation camps are illegal. There had been three cases presented to the Supreme Court regarding the legality of the camps, and, after the third one, the camps were ordered to be shut down. The first two cases, brought forth by a Nisei university student and a man who evaded Manzanar to stay with his girlfriend who was Caucasian, had no effect on the court despite the good argument that no Italian-Americans or German-Americans were relocated. The third suit is brought forth by a Nisei woman who protests the detaining of loyal citizens against their will. The court rules in favor of the woman and the military, anticipating this outcome, announces that they will shut the camps down within the next twelve months. The Japanese living in the camps are not nearly as happy as they should be because most of them have nowhere to go once the camps are shut down, and they fear that they will not be accepted by the public wherever they may go due to war prejudice. There has been an emergence of anti-Japanese groups and societies all along the west coast to discourage the Japanese from settling there, and many of the people in camps will not be able to afford traveling off the west coast to live. Despite the fact that most Japanese do not have a problem resettling after leaving camp, those who remain in camp are fearful because they hear horror stories. Jeanne has never thought the outside world was a bad place until she began hearing the stories, but now she has to prepare herself to be hated by the whole country. Despite the fact that the older children mostly move back to the east coast, they know that Papa never will. Jeanne likens Papa's attitude as that of a slave who has been freed but does not know what to do with his life because he has always been a slave.

Chapter Seventeen

In preparation for the camps closing the schools shut down in June 1945 and release one final yearbook. The farms end production as well, and the farm equipment is auctioned off. It is announced that the camp will be closed by December 1, and those who do not remove themselves from camp by that date will be resettled by the government, either in a place of their choosing or in their old neighborhoods. Papa refuses to move the family and decides that the government will have to choose where the Wakatsuki family will live. Papa will no longer be able to work as a fisherman in the real world because his boats were taken away and a law has been passed that says Issei, Japanese Americans who are not US citizens, cannot hold fishing licenses. Papa is disgusted by news of the Japanese relocation and the war in general. Papa's stubbornness does not pay off because by the time they leave camp all of the housing has been taken, and they have a hard time finding a place to live; this is something Mama and Papa often argue about, placing the blame on one another. Papa has a plan to ask the government to give the returning Japanese a loan to build their own housing development, sure that they deserve it after the way they have been treated, but Mama does not think it will happen. In August of 1945 the war officially ends when the US drops a bomb on Hiroshima, which ends any hope the remaining campers have of staying in the camps until they find a place to live. The Japanese rejoice that they are no longer the enemy, but Papa thinks of his family back in Hiroshima and waits

patiently for the day his family is removed from
Manzanar in October 1945.

Chapter Eighteen

About one year after the bombing of Hiroshima Woody visits Papa's family. His great-aunt Toyo shows him the damage caused by the bomb, including tombstones that are tilted and nearly tipped over or destroyed. Toyo says that only one member of the family was killed in the blast, but she does not want to discuss it. Toyo shows Woody his father's tombstone with the date of death listed as 1913. Woody tells Toyo that his father is alive and well in California, but Toyo maintains that to her family he was declared dead in 1913 after they had not heard from him in nine years. Toyo is happy to hear that Papa is alive and says that her sorrow over the devastation of the war has diminished at the news of his survival. At first Woody is scared to visit Papa's family in Hiroshima because he is a part of the American military, but he brings fifty pounds of sugar because he knows that it is in short supply there. The family immediately sees that Woody is his father's son and welcomes him, regardless of his position in the American military. The family lives in a very nice home though there is little left in the home as they have had to sell most of their things for money in the wake of the war, though they share what little food and sake they have with Woody. Woody is glad that the stories Papa has been telling about his family all these years have been true and he thinks that Papa would be proud of the way his family has treated Woody. As Woody is about to sleep, he hears someone crying next to him and sees that it is Toyo; she says he looks just like his father and then she leaves. Woody thinks Toyo and Papa look alike and thinks he should have asked Toyo about him, vowing to remember to do so the next day and also to climb a hill that Papa used to climb when he was younger.

Chapter Nineteen

Papa decides what is left of the family must leave Manzanar with style and so despite Mama's protests he goes to a nearby town to buy a car. He buys the most unique car that he can find, a Nash that is dark blue and has a gearshift in the dashboard. The nine members of the family who are left are transported over four days and three trips back to Long Beach with whatever belongings they have acquired over their time at Manzanar. The car is not very reliable and manages to break down every one hundred miles or so, but Papa proves to be quite the mechanic and always fixes the problem. Papa drinks for most of the trip but sobers up just before they arrive as though he is preparing himself for a confrontation. Jeanne prepares herself to be hated, as though hatred is going to come rushing at her, and she is scared of it because of the way she has heard the adults talking; but Jeanne is relieved when she gets back home to see that nothing has really changed at all. There are not many places available for the Japanese to live in but the Wakatsukis manage to find a three-bedroom apartment in a housing project in Long Beach with the aid of the American Friends Service. The family is very happy to finally have a private toilet as well as a kitchen, but they are sad to find out that most of their furniture that had been stored is missing, as are Papa's boats. Papa manages to cling to the hope that the government will provide money for the returning Japanese to build their own housing development though Mama, thinking realistically, gets a job. Papa is too proud to work in a cannery, but Mama is not as she knows the family needs it, so that is what she does. Jeanne feels as though the hatred everyone was worried about may not be coming at all.

Chapter Twenty

Jeanne enjoys her sixth grade teacher and does not feel discrimination until a day when she is asked to read aloud in class. While Jeanne is reading the class stares at her in awe, and a girl named Radine tells Jeanne she did not think she would speak English. Jeanne realizes that people probably will not hate her for being Japanese but they will see her as a foreigner despite the fact that she was born in America. She thinks that the relocation and deportation of the Japanese happened as much from white ignorance as from Japanese passivity and acceptance of being discriminated against. Part of Jeanne wants to disappear, but she also desperately wants to be accepted so she joins many school groups and clubs. Outside of school Jeanne realizes that there are some children who are not allowed to be her friend because their parents will not allow it. Jeanne asks Radine if she can be in the Girl Scouts with her but Radine's mother, who is troop leader, refuses to allow Jeanne to join. Jeanne and Radine manage to become friends anyway, and Jeanne teaches Radine how to twirl a baton. The girls together join a Boy Scouts drum and bugle corps as baton twirlers, and Jeanne is made majorette, which means she leads the group while wearing a white outfit. Jeanne realizes that the boys accept her because they like to see girls wearing tight outfits and it is at this point when she sees how powerful a tool her sexuality can be. When Woody and Ray return from the military they are proud of Jeanne but Papa is not, he feels as though she should make an effort to be more Japanese. Jeanne begins to lose respect for Papa because he refuses to conform to American norms and values, and the family is still stuck in a cramped apartment due to Papa's stubbornness. Jeanne is embarrassed by Papa when he comes to a PTA awards dinner and bows to the crowds in a Japanese fashion.

Chapter Twenty-One

Jeanne begins to move away from her Japanese ancestry and embrace her friendship with Radine. They are close friends because they are social equals because Radine's family is poor and they live in the ghetto, and also they have the same interests and hobbies. However, when the girls start at Long Beach Polytechnic High School Jeanne begins to see the differences between herself and Radine. Jeanne is not given the same fair treatment in the band as Radine is and the boys that both girls are interested in go after Radine and only flirt with Jeanne. She begins to resent her father more than ever before because she feels as though his insistence on embracing his Japanese heritage is what sets her apart from the other kids in her school. All Jeanne wants is to be accepted, and as she gets increasingly frustrated she begins to hang out on the streets, and nearly drops out of school. Papa decides to begin farming again after he has a near-death experience from drinking too much. He moves the family to Santa Monica Valley where he works as a sharecropper on a strawberry farm. It is Jeanne's senior year, and she is determined to fit in with her new classmates. In the spring, she is nominated as the carnival queen, and when it comes to election day she dresses in a sarong with a hibiscus flower in her hair, rather in the typical sock-hop outfits popular in the 1950's. It is obvious by the applause that Jeanne will win, but the teachers, determined to not allow it, try to stuff the ballot box. Jeanne's friend Leonard exposes the teachers' plans and Jeanne wins. Papa is angry about Jeanne's use of sexuality to attract white boys and worries that she will marry one someday so he forces her to take Japanese dance lessons, and in return he allows to her keep her position as carnival queen. Jeanne wears a conservative dress to the coronation ceremony, and though she receives compliments she hears people talking about her as she walks by. She realizes she never should have tried to be someone she is not because no matter what she will not be invited to the white girls' parties because her face is Japanese. She wonders if she has any idea who she really is.

Chapter Twenty-Two

Jeanne ends up being the first member of her family
to marry a non-Japanese person and also the first to
graduate from college. She has a hard time believing
that Manzanar ever existed because the Japanese
people never talk about it and those who are not
Japanese have never heard of it. She never speaks
about it until she meets a white woman in 1966 who
was a photographer at Manzanar. In 1972 Jeanne
returns to Manzanar with her husband and three
children though she almost does not recognize it. She
cannot believe how close the camp was to a highway
though she does remember the fruit trees that lined
the property. The camp is in ruins now and there are
only a few buildings still standing. Jeanne thinks of
Mama, who had died seven years prior, remembers
the voices she had heard throughout the camp. Jeanne
begins to remember rock gardens and glee club and
surveys the ruins like an archeological site. Jeanne
recalls that her life began there while Papa's ended
and in the years since her visit she manages to forget
Manzanar almost entirely, though it is not her wish to
forget it but to move on from it. Jeanne remembers
the night Papa took them from camp in the old blue
Nash, driving around drunk and on flat tires, nearly
running over the families leaving camp; but Jeanne
had total faith that her father would get them out from
under the black cloud of hatred that hung over them.

About BookCaps

We all need refreshers every now and then. Whether you are a student trying to cram for that big final, or someone just trying to understand a book more, BookCaps can help. We are a small, but growing company, and are adding titles every month.

Visit www.bookcaps.com to see more of our books, or contact us with any questions.

Made in the USA
Lexington, KY
17 January 2013